BLOHM & VOSS

Bv 222 "Wiking" – Bv 238

Heinz J. Nowarra

Schiffer Military History
Atglen, PA

Sources:

Nowarra-Kens, Die Deutschen Flugzeuge 1933-1945
Smithsonian Institution, National Air and Space Museum, Washington, D.C.
US Naval Air Test Center, Patuxent River, Md.

Photo Credits:

Koblenz Federal Archives (BA)
Nowarra
Smithsonian Institution
National Air and Space Museum
Aders

Translated from the German by Don Cox.
Cover artwork by Steve Ferguson.

Printed in China.
ISBN: 0-7643-0295-7

This book was originally published under the title,
Luftgiganten über See: Bv 222 Wiking - Bv 238,
by Podzun-Pallas Verlag.

We are interested in hearing from authors with book ideas on related topics.

Published by Schiffer Publishing Ltd.
4880 Lower Valley Road
Atglen, PA 19310
Phone: (610) 593-1777
FAX: (610) 593-2002
E-mail: Schifferbk@aol.com.
Please write for a free catalog.
This book may be purchased from the publisher.
Please include $3.95 postage.
Try your bookstore first.

Bv 222 V 1, already wearing Luftwaffe markings of X4+AH, during flight testing.

Above: Bv 222 V 1, D-ANTE, posing in front of the hangar where it had just been built.
Below: The flying boat after its maiden flight.

Blohm & Voss Bv 222

As with many other famous aircraft of the Second World War, such as the Heinkel He 70 and He 111, the six-engine Bv 222 and 238 flying boats owe their existence to an initiative of the Deutsche Lufthansa. Lufthansa's technical branch published the basic requirements for a large flying boat which would be used for commercial transatlantic routes.

This requirement was passed to the firms of Heinkel, Dornier and Blohm & Voss (formerly the Hamburger Flugzeugbau). Heinkel had considerable experience in building maritime aircraft, as did Dornier with flying boats, and Blohm & Voss had paved a new path in seaplane construction with their Ha 139. With the Do X from 1929, Dornier had shown how such "flying ships" could be build. At the time, however, there was still a lack of suitable engines.

Heinkel believed it could manage with four engines and offered the He 120, later designated the He 220. Dornier leaned toward the design of the Do X with its Do 20 proposal, but wanted to fit paired engines. Eight diesel motors would provide the power to four airscrews. Dr. Vogt, the chief of design at Blohm & Voss, wanted to install six engines from the beginning, using the reliable BMW 132.

Lufthansa considered Vogt's proposal to have the most merit. A contract was issued on 19 August 1937 for three of the flying boats, designated the Ha (later Bv) 222. Comprehensive tow basin testing got underway at the Deutsche Schiffsbau Versuchsanstalt (German Shipbuilding Test Facility).

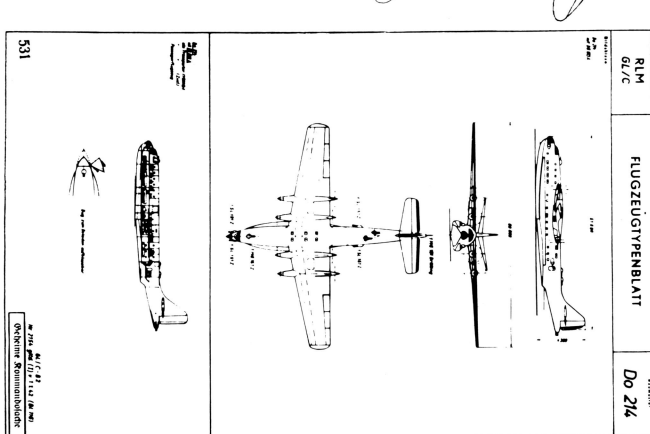

Above:
Draft sketch for the Heinkel He 120, later known as the He 220.

Right:
RLM (GL/C) aircraft type leaflet for the Dornier Do 214, of which only one flying model was built.

Corner seating in one of the DLH Bv 222's compartments.

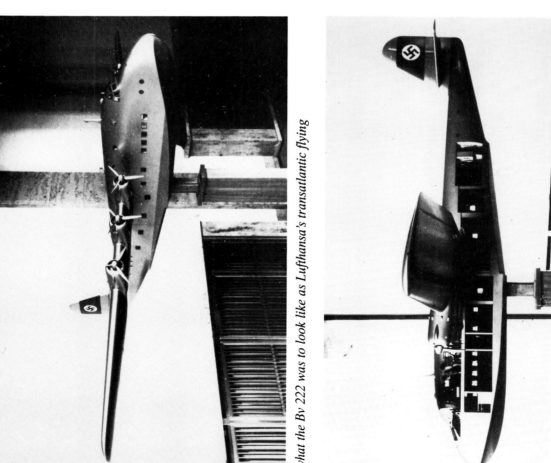

This was what the Bv 222 was to look like as Lufthansa's transatlantic flying boat.

Cutaway model of the DLH Bv 222 showing cabin layout.

In December Lufthansa formulated the contract in more detail: with a takeoff weight of 45,000 kg the flying boat was to carry 24 passengers by day and 16 by night in sleeping compartments across the Atlantic.

In January 1938 design work began, with construction starting on the Bv 222 V 1 in September of that year. Work started on the V 2 and V 3 just a few weeks later. It was obvious that construction of such large flying boats, on which no prior experience could be drawn, would take considerable time. In addition, the outbreak of World War Two drew skilled labor away from the program to support the more critical Bv 138 program. Nevertheless, construction work continued on the Bv 222.

On 16 July representatives from Lufthansa viewed the mockup for the aircraft's interior layout and demanded changes. Once these were carried out the mockup was approved on 7 August 1940. By this time, however, all participants were aware that Lufthansa would never receive these boats, since the Luftwaffe was in urgent need of transport capacity. At the end of August Bv 222 V 1 entered the final stage of assembly. After completing its flotation testing and taxi trials, the monstrous machine took off on its maiden flight on 7 September 1940, flown by Captain Helmut Wasa Rodig. Factory testing revealed that flight handling characteristics were satisfactory, although the flying boat had a tendency to become instable in horizontal flight and, when taxiing on water, began to lurch from side to side.

Left: Bv 222 V 1, X4+AH, over the mouth of the Elbe River during factory testing.

Bv 222 on land with open loading ramp. (BA)

Bv 222 V 1: the assembly worker to the right and below gives a good idea of the flying boat's monstrous size. The navigation cupola can be made out above the pilot's compartment.

The powerplants for the Bv 222 V 1 through V 6 and V 8 were nearly identical: 2x3 BMW Bramo 323 Rs with a takeoff performance of 1,000 hp each.

Bv 222. Its wingspan was a full 46 meters! (BA)

These soldiers curiously eye the flying behemoth, which would shortly ferry them to one of the islands in the Aegean Sea.

Until December of 1940 the airplane was repeatedly flown and tweaked, until testing had to be broken off due to the buildup of ice on the Elbe. In order not to squander away the fuel needed for testing, the Luftwaffe proposed conducting a long-range transport testing program between Hamburg and Kirkenes.

Blohm & Voss agreed. The Bv 222 V 1 was now given a military camouflage paint scheme and registered as CC+EQ. The evaluation program proved successful. By 19 August 1941 the flying boat had completed seven flights along the above-named flight route. In 120 hours of actual flight time 65,000 kg of supplies had been delivered to Kirkenes and 221 wounded personnel brought home again. Total distance was 30,000 km.

There then followed a general overhaul prior to setting out for Athens, from where the aircraft would ferry supplies to the Afrikakops in Derna.

The growth of barnacles on the hull necessitated a return to Hamburg. Subsequently, between 16 October and 6 November 1941 the Bv 222 V 1 flew the Athens-Derna route seventeen times, bringing 30,000 kg to Libya and returning with 515 wounded personnel on board. Since the aircraft had not yet been fitted with armament the crew still belonged to Blohm & Voss escort was provided by two Bf 110s.

While the upper picture shows the Bv 222 V 1 still without armament, the lower one reveals the weapons cupolas on the fuselage spine. (BA)

Results of this second operational evaluation showed that the lurching tendency had not yet been fully eliminated and that the powerplants (instead of the BMW 132, more powerful 200 ho Bramo 323 engines had been fitted) did not always function properly. Its performance, however, was acceptable. Maximum speed was 385 km/h at 4,500 meters, maximum range being 7,000 km. (The flying boat could have therefore flown from Hamburg to New York non-stop). Regarding transport, the Bv 222 V 1 could carry 92 fully equipped infantry soldiers or 72 wounded on stretchers.

In the winter of 1941/42 the boat was given a complete overhaul in Hamburg and fitted with defensive weapons. These consisted of an MG 81 in the nose, two DL 131 turrets firing MG 131s along the upper fuselage and four MG 81s in side stations. The Bv 222 V 1 was also given a new registration code, X4+AH, and formed the basis of Luft-Transport-Staffel (LTS, Air Transport Sq.) 222. Accordingly, it carried the code "S 1" on its rudder. Following this, the flying boat was continually in action in the Mediterranean theater, even surviving an attack by three Beaufighters on a flight from Taranto to Tripoli, until being lost in the Athens harbor after colliding with a wreck lying just under the water's surface. The boat was forced to set down on the water in total darkness due to an air raid alarm, so that the pilot didn't see the marker buoys. The wreck ripped to hull open and X4+AH sank within a few minutes in mid-February 1943.

Above: Loading the Bv 222 V 1 in the harbor of Tripoli.
Below: Bv 222 V 1 sinking after its collision in the harbor of Piraeus.

Bv 222 V 2, Werknr. 366, (initially coded CC+ER) carried out its first flight on 7 August 1941 and was taken over by LTS 222 on 10 August 1942 after a thorough flight testing program. Since the aircraft was initially planned as a long-range patrol flying boat for Fliegerführer Atlantik, it was fitted with two supplemental gunner's stations slung beneath the wings, each with two MG 131 machine guns. This was in addition to the standard armament as carried on the V 1. However, testing at Travemünde showed that the additional air resistance caused a significant loss in speed and they were eventually removed.

In the interim the third boat, Bv 222 V 3 (Werkr. 439, initial coding DM+SD), had been integrated into LTS 222 as early as 9 December 1941, having just completed its first flight on the preceding 28 November. With the Luftwaffe it was registered as X4+CH. Between January and March of 1942 Bv 222 V 3 carried out 21 supply missions between Taranto and Brindisi to Tripoli. LTS 222 considered the defensive armament non-essential and dispensed with all weaponry aside from the nose-mounted MG 81. After the accident with the Bv 222 V 1, V 3 returned to Hamburg, was fitted with a more comprehensive armament suite and resubordinated to Fliegerführer Atlantik. In June of 1943 it was caught by British fighter-bombers in the Biscarosse Roads in France and destroyed.

Bv 222 V 2 was also active in the long-range reconnaissance role over the Atlantic, eventually deploying to Norway. There it was discovered at anchor in 1945.

Left: Bv 222 V 2 still wearing its initial registration code of CC+ER and with the gunners' gondolas beneath the wings (later removed).

Bv 222 V 2 with the new X4+BH coding, shortly before being operationally deployed. Notice the rear turret on the upper fuselage.

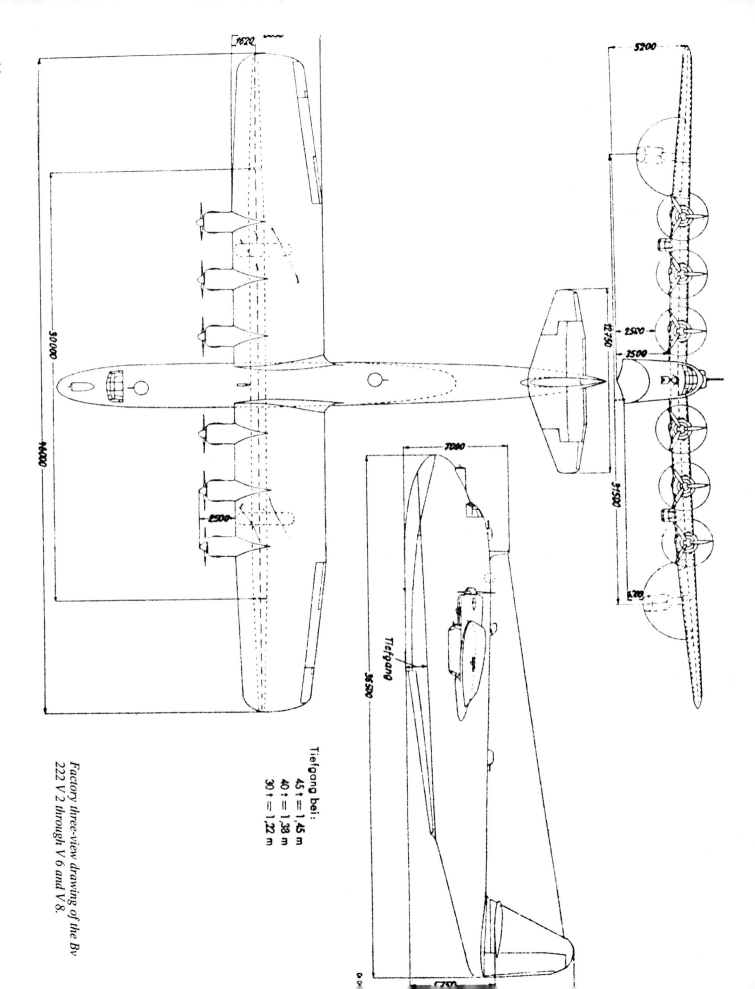

Tiefgang bei:
45 t = 1,45 m
40 t = 1,38 m
30 t = 1,22 m

Factory three-view drawing of the Bv 222 V 2 through V 6 and V 8.

Above: Bv 222 V 2 after having the gondolas removed, having its engines worked on.
Below: Bv 222 V 2 in the fjord of Sörreisa near Bardufoss, Norway, 1945.

Pilot's compartment in the Bv 222 V 1. The officers are from the Erprobungsstelle Travemünde and are responsible for accepting the aircraft.

Radio and engineering compartment within the Bv 222 V 2. Radio equipment consisted of a Lorenz VP 257 long wave transceiver and a Lorenz VP 245 transoceanic relay set.

Interior view of the Bv 222 V 2 hull; this is Compartment C.

Bv 222 V 2 during repairs on the hull bottom, in Piraeus on 16 December 1941.

Frontal view of a Bv 222.

Rear view of a Bv 222.

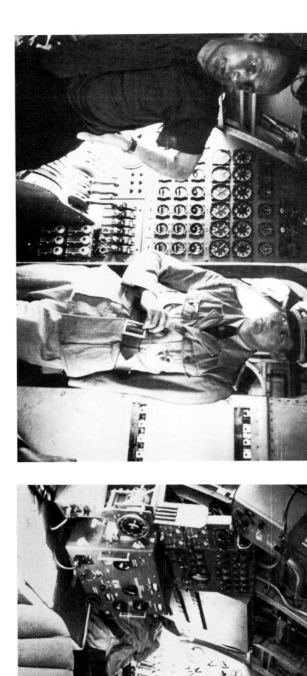

The Bv 222 V 2 flew with Lufthansa engineer Dilewitsch (left) as its on-board engineer. The officer standing in the entryway is a member of the Erprobungsstelle (or Test Facility) Travemünde.

Two other officers from the test facility in the radio and engineering room of the Bv 222 V 2. Below: Bv 222 V 1 on its maiden flight.

It was also called the Wiking (Viking). Appropriately, then, the markings of Luftransportgruppe See 222 took the form of a Viking longboat. (BA)

The Bv 222 was particularly well-suited for Atlantic operations as long as the enemy didn't have adequate support from aircraft carriers. With reduced speed, the flying boat could remain airborne for an incredible 33 hours. In addition to having its defensive armament beefed up, the boats were also fitted with the most modern electronic equipment available to Germany: the FuG 200 Hohentwiel surface search radar, the FuG 16 for command guided target approach, the FuG 25 A Identification Friend or Foe(IFF) system and the FuG 101 A radio altimeter.

These aircraft were armed with two MG 151s in DL 151 turrets on the boat's upper fuselage, two MG 81 guns each in side positions and an MG 131 in the forward starboard nose position. The installation of this armament and antenna equipment limited their top speed to 294 km/h.

In 1942 LTS 222 received an additional four flying boats, which can be considered the Bv 222 A-series: V 4 X4+DH on 20 April 1942, V 5 X4+EH on 7 July 1942, V 6 X4+FH on 21 August 1942 and V 8 X4+HH on 26 September 1942.

Above:
Bv 222 V 3, X4+CH.
Center: Bv 222 V 2, CC+ER, shortly after being built and just before taking to water for the first time. The gunners' gondola can be seen just below the outer engine.
Below:
Front view of the Bv 222 V 3.

The Bv 222's support floats. As can be clearly seen, the floats were divided into two halves which retracted outward and upward.

Nose of the Bv 222 V 6, X4+EH, from above. Gun turrets have not yet been completed.

Above and above right:
Bv 222 V 4, X4+DH, during final equipment fitting.

Right:
In front of the hangar at Hamburg-Finkenwerder. Weapons installation has not yet taken place.

Turret and MG 151 on the upper wing of Bv 222 V 4.

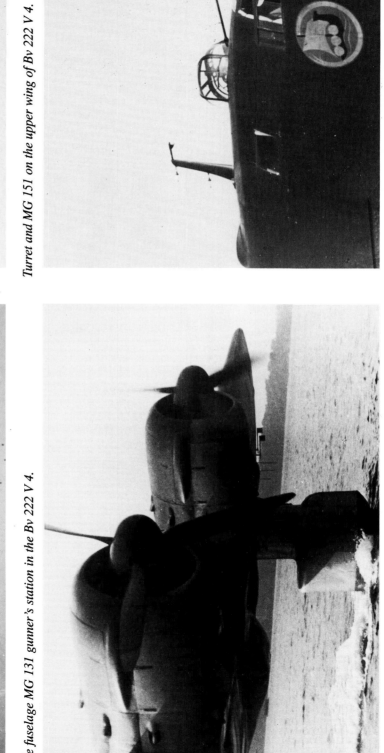

Turret and MG 151 behind the cockpit on Bv 222 V 4. Notice the Staffel badge of LTS 222.

Side fuselage MG 131 gunner's station in the Bv 222 V 4.

Outer engines and support floats on Bv 222 V 4.

Bv 222 V 1 (foreground) and Bv 222 V 5, X4+EH, in the Piraeus Roads.

Bv 222 V 4 was fitted with a new horizontal stabilizer which was to have been used as a testbed for the follow-on Bv 238. It flew with LTS 222, delivering supplies to the Afrikakorps, and on 10 December 1942 was twice seriously damaged in an attack in which Bv 222 V 1 was also involved. Despite this, it managed to reach its destination. Together with the V 2, it then began Atlantic long-range reconnaissance patrols. In October the two aircraft met up with an Avro Lancaster over the ocean. One of the two managed to shoot down the British four-engine bomber. Bv 222 V 4 remained in service through to 1945 and, just shortly after the cease-fire, was sunk by its own crew in the harbor of Kiel-Holtenau.

Bv 222 V 5 also was initially employed flying supplies in the Mediterranean, but after the V 1's accident, too, was called back home and structurally reinforced and at the same time fitted with stronger defensive armament at Lufthansa's docks in Travemünde. In April of 1943 V 5 was assigned to Fliegerführer Atlantik, but in June of that year was destroyed along with V 3 by British fighter-bombers outside of Biscarosse.

Of the flying boats, Bv 222 V 6 must certainly have had the shortest lifespan. Entering service on 21 August 1942 with LTS 222, the boat was caught in the open by British Beaufighters south of the island of Pantelleria on its way from Taranto to Tripoli and shot down in flames.

Kampfgeschwader zbV 2, which included LTS 222, ordered a change in flight routes as a countermeasure. However, since the Bv 222s flew precisely according to plan, it didn't take long for British patrol aircraft to determine at what point these flying boats would pass within range of their strike fighters. From then on, it was simply a matter of the British intercepting the Tripoli-bound transports bringing supplies in to Rommel's forces. The returning aircraft, which only carried wounded on board, were not attacked.

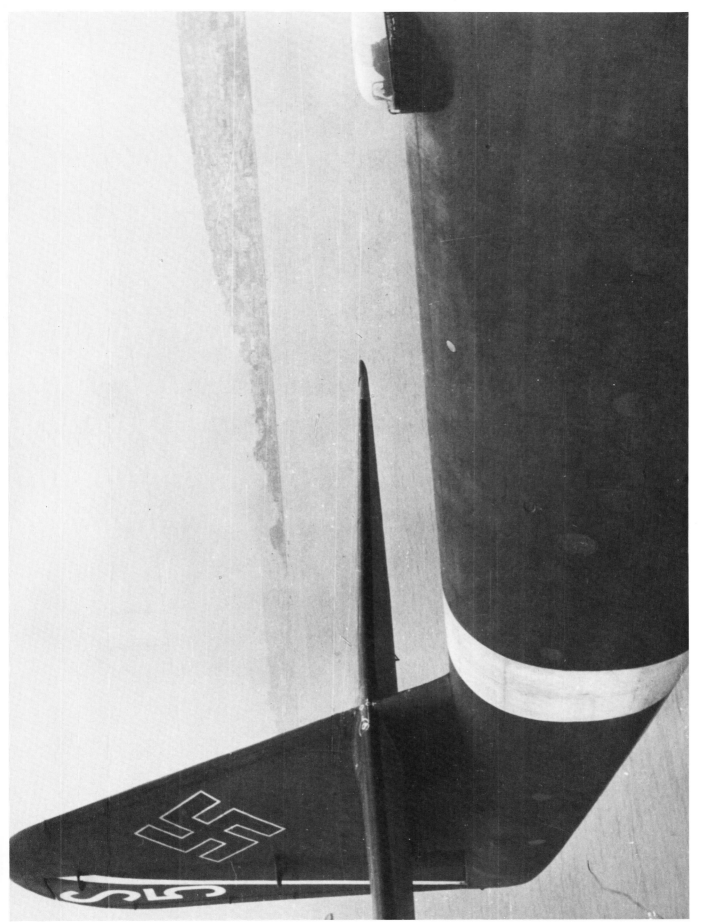

Empennage showing rudder and DL 131 turret of Bv 222 V 5.

Above: Bv 222 V 5 in the Mediterranean.

Below: The same boat with polar camouflage in northern Norway.

Bv 222 Wiking in flight over northern Germany. (BA)

Bv 222 V 7, TB+QL, moving down the slipway after final assembly.

On the morning of 10 December 1942 Bv 222 V 1, V 4 and V 8 were flying at an altitude of just five meters above sea level. But the British flew even lower. From an altitude of only two meters above the glassy smooth sea they pulled up into the giant boats' V-formation. The three boats tried to provide protective cover for each other. As mentioned previously, only V 1 escaped unscathed; V 4 suffered damage, but remained in the air; Bv 222 V 8 was hit so bad, however, that it could no longer stay aloft. It exploded upon impact with the water. Following this incident the commander of LTS 222, Hauptmann Führer, declared that the Bv 222's armament was evidently too weak. After the loss of V 3 and V 5 outside of Biscarosse, only V 2 and V 4 were left available for operations with Fliegerführer Atlantik.

The planned Bv 222 B remained only a project for a civil version. In order to increase the Bv 222's range even more, Bv 222 V 7 (TB+QL) was fitted with diesel Jumo 207 C engines having a continuous output of 680 hp and emergency power of 750 hp. The Jumo 207 proved to be a temperamental powerplant, however, with a tendency to cut out. Nevertheless, the Bv 222 V 7 which is considered the prototype for the C-series was able to achieve a range of 6,100 km with a takeoff weight of 50,000 kg. The V 7's first flight took place on 1 April 1943. On 16 August 1943 Fliegerführer Atlantik assumed ownership of the machine, which served until the war's end and was sunk by its own crew in 1945 outside of Travemünde.

Only nine C-0 series aircraft were laid down, of which only five were completed. Of these, 014 through 017 were to have formed a new D-0 series with Jumo 207 D engines. This was never implemented, however, since Junkers could not make the Jumo 207 D reliable enough for operational use.

Bv 222 V 7 after its maiden flight.

Bv 222 V 7 shortly before being lowered into the water.

Bv 222 V 7. This photo shows the different appearance of this Bv 222 caused by its new engines. Note the position of the CH coding on the hull.

View looking toward the forward fuselage and wing gun stations.

Above: Bv 222 V 2. Below: Bv 222 V 7 during factory flight testing on the lower Elbe.

Bv 222 C-09 was assigned to Fliegerführer Atlantik on 23 July 1943 and, after Germany's retreat from France, continued to operate from Norwegian bases in the long-range reconnaissance role. In 1945 it was destroyed at Travemünde by British Hawker Typhoons. C-011 fell into American hands undamaged and was flown to the United States for evaluation. Following an extensive testing program, which resulted in the American aviation industry being provided with much useful information on the design of such large flying boats, the airplane was scrapped. Construction of the eight-engine Hughes Hercules flying boat may have been stimulated by this information.

Bv 222 C-012 suffered a similar fate as that of C-011, but this boat was captured in Norway and flown to England by the British despite an engine failure. The British, too, followed the concept of the large flying boat and built the eight-engine Saunders-Roe Princess. The advent of the jet engine, however, made these designs obsolete. The last Bv 222 flying boat was C-013. Although built, it was never put into action, was captured by the Americans and suffered the same fate as C-011. O14 through 017 became victims of the construction halt brought on by the emergency fighter program.

Above: Bv 222 V 7.
Center: Bv 222 V 8, X4+HH, during its delivery on 26 November 1943.
Below: Bv 222 V 8 during operations in the Mediterranean Theater.

Bv 222 V 8 in Finkenwerder on the ramp.

The white band around the rear fuselage indicated this aircraft's planned use in the Mediterranean.

Bv 222 V 8 in the Med, ready for takeoff. Notice the markings of LTS 222 on the nose below the cockpit.

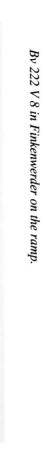

Bv 222 V 8 shortly before setting down, seen during a test flight.

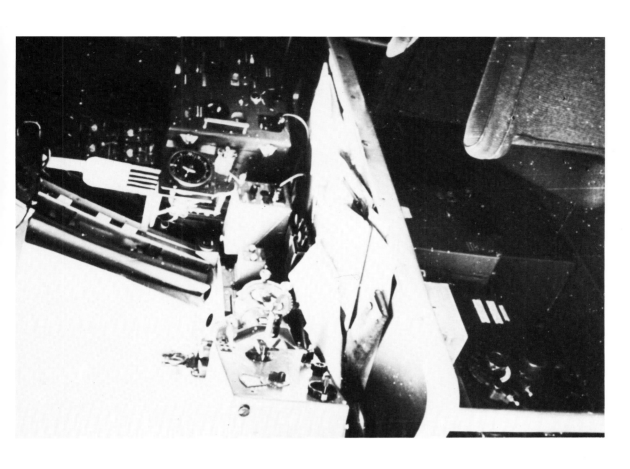

Above left: Radio compartment in a Bv 222 showing rear gunner's position. The catch bag for expended shells hangs below.

Left: Radio officer and his equipment: VP 245 transoceanic receiver and 170 watt VP 257 long wave set.
Above: The radioman's station in a Bv 222.

The last German crew of Bv 222 V 2, minus commander Hauptmann Möhring: (from right) Lt. Steinbach, Lt. Warninghof, OFw Pausinger, remainder unknown.

The US crew which flew the machine to the USA. Pilot was Cmdr. H.E. McNeely; engineer Lt.Cmdr. G.M. Hebert, both of the U.S. Navy.

Bv 222 V 2 after the capitulation in 1945, at rest in Trondheim Fjord. Nationality markings have already been overpainted and British roundels painted on, since the aircraft was first accepted by the English.

Model PV-222 Airplane
At Loading Ramp, Trondheim
Trondheim Fjord, Norway

CONFIDENTIAL
OFFICIAL NAVY PHOTOGRAPH
NOT FOR PUBLICAT

PHOTO PV 26305
8/21/45

The end of the giant flying boats: the German crew of Bv 222 V 2 deboards after handing the boat over to the Americans in Trondheim Fjord.

Blohm & Voss Bv 238

As early as 1940 Dr. Vogt began design work on an eight-engine flying boat for Lufthansa, which was expected to carry 120 passengers over a distance of 8,600 kilometers. It was designated the P.200. But by January 1941 the RLM put a halt to the development and demanded a design for a large multi-role flying boat which would be powered by four Jumo 223 diesel engines of 2,500 hp each. However, since these engines never achieved operational maturity, the project was dropped.

In July of 1941 Dr. Vogt submitted a reworked design which was virtually an enlarged Bv 222. Plans called for using six Daimler-Benz DB 603 engines in the first three boats and six BMW 801s in the fourth aircraft. The flying boat was given type designation Bv 238. A small-scale flying model was to be built in order to avoid difficulties in the prototype's construction. Construction of the model took place at the Flugtechnische Fertigungsgemeinschaft GmbH in Prague. The project was assigned type designation FG 227.

Construction itself was to have been undertaken by Czech students working with the German Dipl.Ing. Ludwig Karch, one of the most renowned glider pilots of the day. The FG 227 was a cantilever, shoulder-wing design with a keeled hull and raised tailplane. Six ILO two-stroke FL 2/400 engines provided the power, each having an output of 21 hp. For flight testing, which was to have initially taken place over land, the airframe was fitted with twin wheels in the nose and tandem wheel landing gears on either side of the fuselage. The aircraft was coded BQ+UZ. Sabotage prevented the first flight from taking place until September 1944, which ended in a crash landing.

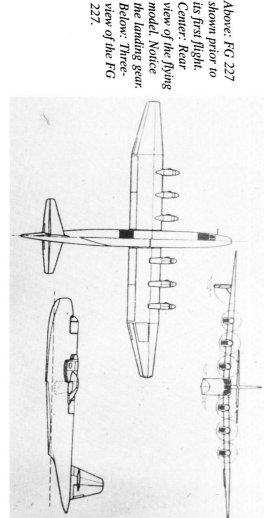

Above: FG 227 shown prior to its first flight. Center: Rear view of the flying model. Notice the landing gear. Below: Three-view of the FG 227.

Above: Close-up photo showing the coding on FG 227.
Below: View of the starbord engines.

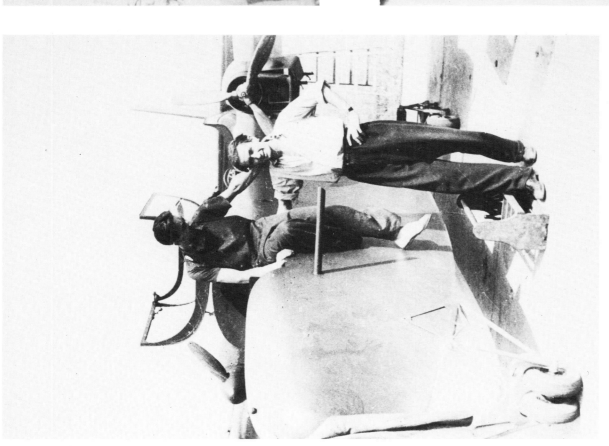

Above:
Two colleagues of the construction team with the FG 227. The diminutive size of the model is shown here to good effect.

The FG 227, therefore, played no role in influencing the development of the Bv 238. Component production and building of jigs for the Bv 238 V 1 began as early as 1942, so that by January of 1944 construction could begin in Finkenwerder. Because of the increasing threat of Allied bombing raids completion was delayed until March of 1945. Flight trials produced such outstanding results that, after just four test flights, the airplane was ready for front-line testing even though the boat had not yet been fitted with any type of armament whatsoever. This would have comprised an HD 151 twin-gun turret with two MG 151/20s, two HL 131 V turrets with four MG 131s each and two MG 131 Zs in side stations. Camouflaged, the Bv 238 V 1 lay at rest on the Shaalsee when it was surprised by four American P-51 Mustangs just four days before the war's end and sunk with gunfire. In 1947/48 it was blown up to facilitate easier dismantling.

The individual parts were taken to Hamburg in 1948/49 for scrapping. Bv 238 V 2 and V 3 were under construction when the war ended, but their hull and wing parts were subsequently scrapped.

Landplanes were projected both for the Bv 222 and the Bf 238, differing only in the incorporation of multi-wheeled landing gear. The land version of the Bv 222 was given project number P.187, while that of the Bv 238 was assigned type designation Bf 250. Additional projects of improved flying boats based on this design were still being worked on at the end of World War II.

Above: Bv 238 V 1, RO+EZ, seen before its first flight in April 1944.
Below: Pilot's compartment of the Bv 238 V 1 with control columns and instrument panel.

Above:
Bv 238 V 1: the empennage was significantly altered over that of the Bv 222.

Right:
Bv 238 V 1 anchored to its buoy during flight testing.

Above right:
Bv 238 V 1 sets down on the water at the end of its maiden flight.

Four phases of the Bv 238 V 1 takeoff: 1) the boat begins to taxi (above left); 2) boat seen just before lifting off (above right); 3) just after becoming airborne (below left); 4) and now flying off (below right).

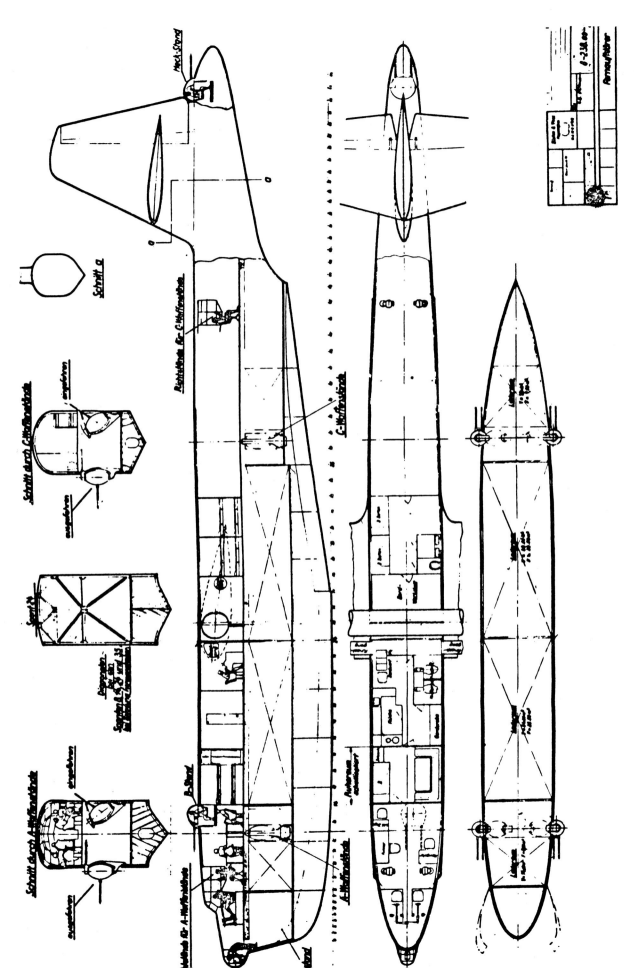

Factory fuselage cutaway drawing of the Bv 238 showing the planned layout for a long-range reconnaissance version.

46

Three-view drawing of a Bv 222-based long-range patrol landplane, developed under the designation P.187.01-01.

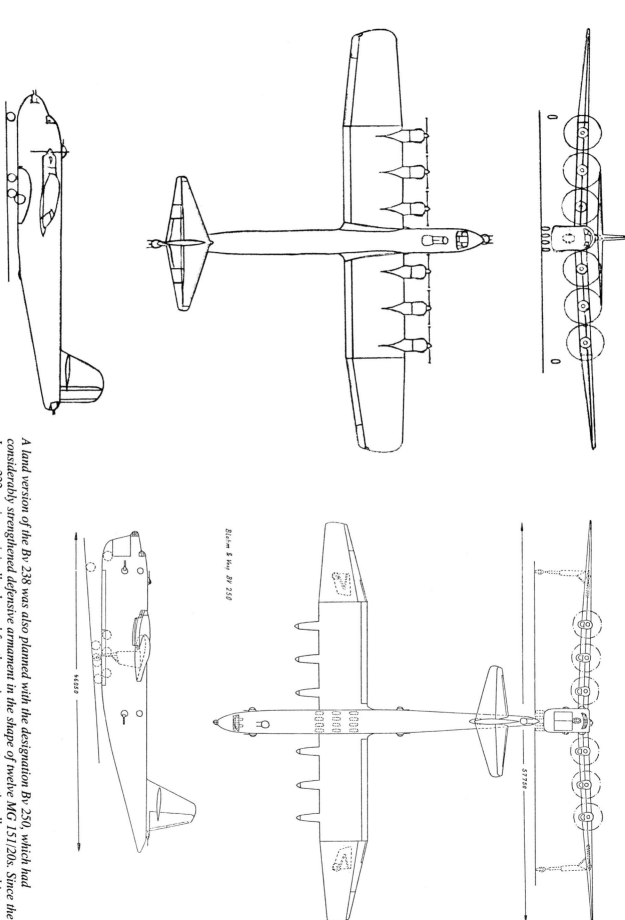

Blohm & Voss BV 250

A land version of the Bv 238 was also planned with the designation Bv 250, which had considerably strengthened defensive armament in the shape of twelve MG 151/20s. Since the Jumo 222 engines originally planned for the project were not operationally mature, this type would have been fitted with the six Daimler-Benz DB 603 engines installed in the Bv 238 V 1. The crew consisted of 11 men. As a troop transport, the machine was expected to carry 150 fully-equipped soldiers.

Technical Data

type	Bv 222 V1	Bv 222 V2-6	Bv 222 V7	FG 227	Bv 238 V1
role	transport	patrol	patrol	test	patrol, transport
crew	6	11	10	1-2	12
engine	Bramo 323R	Bramo 323R	Jumo 207ILO	FL-2	DB 603G
hp	1000/640	1000/620	1000/600	21	2900/1560
wingspan(m)	46.00	46.00	46.00	15.25	60.17
length(m)	36.50	36.50	36.50	12.00	43.36
height(m)	10.90	10.90	10.90	3.54	10.90
wing area(m²)	255	255	255	24.2	362
weight empty(kg)	25,900	27,000	29,680	1,250	54,660
weight gross(kg)	43,500	45,000	45,000	1,640	94,340
load(kg)	17,600	18,000	15,340	-	-
max speed(km/h)	345	345	350	-	355
cruising speed(km/h)	310	320	305	-	335
landing speed(km/h)	125	125	-	-	125
ceiling(m)	6,700	6,500	7,300	-	6,300
range(km)	3100/3400	7000/7450	6100	-	6100
takeoff run(m)	1,000	1,200	1,200	-	-
armament	-	5 MG 81, 6 MG 131	-	4 MG 81, 4 MG 131	-

Above: Bv 238 V 2 hull in the shipyards of the Weserflugzeugbau in Einswarden, 1943. No further work was done on this prototype.
Left:
Bv 238 in flight over the lower Elbe.

Also from the Publisher

HEINKEL He 100

World Record and Propaganda Aircraft

Hans-Peter Dabrowski

Junkers Ju 87

Ulrich Elfrath

MESSERSCHMITT Me 262

Vol.II

The World's First Turbojet Fighter

Manfred Griehl

DORNIER DO 335

"PFEIL"

THE LAST AND BEST PISTON-ENGINE
FIGHTER OF THE LUFTWAFFE

JUNKERS JU 52

Heinz J. Nowarra

MESSERSCHMITT Bf 109

1936-1945

The Bf 109 F (top) of Hans-Joachim Marseille
of JG 27 (above) and the Bf 109 E of Adolf
Galland of JG 26 (foreground).

Heinz J. Nowarra

THE FOCKE-WULF Fw 190

Fighters · Bombers · Ground Attack Aircraft

Heinz J. Nowarra

MESSERSCHMITT Me 163

"Komet"

Vol.II

M. Emmerling/J. Dressel

Ju 88

OVER ALL FRONTS

Joachim Stein